Come to Jesus

Mark 10:13–16
(Jesus Blesses the Children)

by Mary Manz Simon
Illustrated by Dennis Jones

CPH.
SAINT LOUIS

Books by Mary Manz Simon

Hear Me Read Level 1
What Next? CPH
Drip Drop, CPH
Jibber Jabber, CPH
Hide the Baby, CPH
Toot! Toot! CPH
Bing! CPH
Whoops! CPH
Send a Baby, CPH
A Silent Night, CPH
Follow That Star, CPH
Row the Boat, CPH
Rumble, Rumble, CPH
Who Will Help? CPH
Sit Down, CPH
Come to Jesus, CPH
Too Tall, Too Small, CPH
Hurry, Hurry! CPH
Where Is Jesus? CPH

Hear Me Read Level 2
The No-Go King, CPH
Hurray for the Lord's Army! CPH
The Hide-and-Seek Prince, CPH
Daniel and the Tattletales, CPH
The First Christmas, CPH
Through the Roof, CPH
A Walk on the Waves, CPH
Thank You, Jesus, CPH

God's Children Pray, CPH
My First Diary, CPH
52 Ways to Raise Happy, Loving Ki
Thomas Nelson Publishing

Little Visits on the Go, CPH
Little Visits for Toddlers, CPH
Little Visits with Jesus, CPH
Little Visits Every Day, CPH

Copyright © 1992 Concordia Publishing House
3558 S. Jefferson Avenue, St. Louis, MO 63118-3968
Manufactured in the United States of America

Library of Congress Cataloging-in-Publication Data.

Simon, Mary Manz, 1948–
    Come to Jesus : Mark 10:13, Jesus blesses the children / by Mary
Manz Simon ; illustrated by Dennis Jones.
        (Hear me read Bible stories)
    Summary: A simple retelling of the Bible story in which the children
go to see Jesus and be blessed by him.
    ISBN 0-570-04707-2
    1. Bible stories, English—N.T. Mark. 2. Jesus Christ—blessing of
children. 2. Bible stories—N.T.] I. Jones, Dennis, ill. II. Title. III. Series:
Simon, Mary Manz, 1948– Hear me read Bible stories.
BS2401.s45 1992
226.3'09505—dc20   91-7382
                                                                          CIP
                                                                          AC

    3   4   5   6   7   8   9   10   00   99   98   97   96

HEAR · ME · READ

AmberJOY Goodwin
Name

31 May, 1999
Date

Presented by

Mom

To the Adult:

Early readers need two kinds of reading. They need to be read to, and they need to do their own reading. The Hear Me Read Bible Stories series helps you to encourage your child with both kinds.

For example, your child might read this book as you sit together. Listen attentively. Assist gently, if needed. Encourage, be patient, and be very positive about your child's efforts.

Then perhaps you'd like to share the selected Bible story in an easy-to-understand translation or paraphrase.

Using both types of reading gives your child a chance to develop new skills and pride in reading. You share and support your child's excitement.

As a mother and a teacher, I anticipate the joy your child will feel in saying, "Hear me read Bible stories!"

Mary Manz Simon

For Christy
Colossians 3:15–17

1, 2.

2 people.

2 people go to see Jesus.

The child calls,

"We're going to see Jesus.

Hooray! Hooray!"

"Come.

Come with us.

Come with us to see Jesus."

1, 2, 3, 4, 5.

5 people.

5 people go to see Jesus.

The children call,

"We're going to see Jesus."

"Come.

Come with us.

Come with us to see Jesus."

1, 2, 3, 4, 5, 6, 7.

7 people.

7 people go to see Jesus.

The children call,

"We're going to see Jesus.

Hooray! Hooray!"

"Come.

Come with us.

Come with us to see Jesus."

1, 2, 3, 4, 5, 6, 7, 8, 9, 10.

10 people.

10 people go to see Jesus.

The children call,

"We're going to see Jesus.

Hooray! Hooray!"

"Children, see Jesus?

See Jesus?"

"Come.

Come with us.

Jesus will bless the children."

"No.

The children cannot come.

The children cannot
come to see Jesus."

"Come."

About the Author
Mary Manz Simon holds a doctoral degree in education with a specialty in early childhood education. She has taught at levels from preschool through postgraduate. Dr. Simon has also authored *God's Children Pray,* the best-selling *Little Visits with Jesus, Little Visits for Toddlers, Little Visits Every Day, Little Visits on the Go, My First Diary,* and the Hear Me Read Level 2 Bible stories series. She and her husband, the Reverend Henry A. Simon, are the parents of three children.